SUCCESSFUL PROPERTY INVESTMENT

How I turned a £5,000 loan into
£15 million in assets

ELIZABETH BENJAMIN

SUCCESSFUL PROPERTY INVESTMENT - How I turned a £5,000 loan into £15 million in assets

Copyright © 2016 Elizabeth Benjamin

The right of Elizabeth Benjamin to be identified as the Author of the work has been asserted by him in accordance with the Copyright, Designs and Patent Act 1988.

All rights reserved. No part of this publication may be reproduced, stored in a retrieval system or transmitted, in any form or by any means, without the prior written permission of the author, be otherwise circulated in any form of binding or cover, other than that in which it is published. A CIP catalogue record for this title is available from the British Library.

ISBN: 978-1-910090-98-5

Book cover design & layout by: www.madeforministry.co.uk

Printed by: www.madeforministry.co.uk

CONTENTS

Dedication	4
Preface	5
CHAPTER ONE - My Background	9
CHAPTER TWO - Taking Action	13
CHAPTER THREE - Why Property?	19
CHAPTER FOUR - Buying Property	25
CHAPTER FIVE - A Successful Property Magnate	33
CHAPTER SIX - Buying Property Abroad	39
CHAPTER SEVEN - Lessons Learned	43
CHAPTER EIGHT - Make Money, Not Excuses	49
CHAPTER NINE - Right Mind-Set	59
CHAPTER TEN - Wealth Creation	65

DEDICATION

I dedicate this book to my husband. Your strength and help contributes to my development and the success of every project I take on.

To Pastor Matthew Ashimolowo and Mensa Otabil, for helping birth the desire and vision to write this book. You have both influenced my journey and mentored me through your teachings.

PREFACE

The secret about successful real estate investment is that there is no secret. With the right know-how anybody can do it. Property investment is about numbers, it's about land, it's about buildings and it's about providing people with homes and other resources that can only be facilitated through real estate.

Buildings are all around us. No matter where you are in the world, as long as you are on dry land, you will eventually come across a building of some sort. Everyone needs accommodation and the necessity for a place to call home will remain on the earth as long as humans do. Even in the current challenging season for buy-to-let investors, I still believe (using the right strategy to match your goals) property investment is one of the best ways to create wealth. As long as demand continues to rise and cost of ownership is low, there is profit to be made.

I have been inspired by the world around me and the people within it. My faith has kept me grounded and encouraged me to press on when things got difficult and challenges seemed impossible to overcome. I have decided to tell my story because I hold a fundamental belief that anybody can achieve optimal success in property investment irrespective of new government legislation, tax changes or housing policies.

In an edition of *Property Investor News* [1], John Heron, Paragon Director of Mortgages, submitted his views on the impact of the recent higher 3% stamp duty taxes that commence in April 2016 for buy-to-let investors. Heron stated, "It certainly won't be welcomed by investors but does it damage the fundamental benefits of BTL? I would say ***probably not…***" When asked whether the tax is more of a disincentive than a mortgage relief reduction, Heron replied, "They are very different as the tax relief will not affect all landlords but this stamp duty rise impacts all purchases by investors. Ultimately, neither of these changes will stop property investors from buying…" and, "There is nothing in the housing policy that has moved the dial on tenant demand." It is my view that if you desire to help solve the homeless crisis, have a passion to place people in decent accommodation and put people before profit; you can still make a success in property investment.

One of the biggest obstacles people face is fear; because of fear, people are plagued with 'if's' and 'but's' - it prevents them from taking action and starting a new venture. We allow fear to govern the choices we make and the risks we take. We fail to realise that it is fear that pollutes our ability to dream big, realise those dreams and then take advantage of the opportunities that present themselves.

In light of the recent changes, some landlords with small portfolios or one-off properties may choose to sell. Most landlords I have spoken to, especially with large portfolios, will actually consider the changes as an opportunity to buy from those who opt to sell as they are in it for the long hall! Policies come and go but the demand for property is greater than the current supply, meaning there is still a need to be met.

How do you see the world? Are you focused on your current circumstances and the problems you are presently facing, including policies that keep changing? Or are your eyes fixed on a bigger and more important goal? How you see the world determines what your world looks like. If you can change what you see then you can change what you experience - and if you can change what you experience then you can transform your reality into something bigger, better and brighter.

Everything that I am currently doing and everything that I have achieved so far has not happened by accident. I came from a working class background yet still made a success in property investment; turning a £5k overdraft into over £15m in assets.

If you have a dream or are yet to dream, then join me as I narrate my journey. Discover the challenges I faced, the lessons I learned and the obstacles I overcame along the way. Now is not the time to put things off. Do not delay or side-line your ambitions. Think of it this way; what would you do and how would you behave if you knew you could make your life a success?

Real estate investment is exciting, rewarding and lucrative when done correctly; that's what this book is about. If you desire to change your current reality through property investment then read on!

8

Chapter One
MY BACKGROUND

In the 90's, as a mother who was juggling a couple of jobs and studying whilst raising four children, my situation was no different to many today who are forced to work several jobs but still required to make time for other responsibilities. I did not have an 'advantage' growing up and I do not come from a 'privileged' background. The only thing that separates me from those who fail to achieve their dreams are the choices I have made and continue to make.

If someone had told me several years ago that I would be running my own businesses, mentoring, advising others on property and investment and writing books, I would have called them a liar – not because I didn't think I was capable but simply because the thought had never really crossed my mind. I wanted to be successful, I wanted to improve my life and provide my children with the opportunities I didn't have as a child. I wanted to raise them in an environment that was foreign to the one I grew up in. Whilst I knew what I wanted to achieve – I did not know how I could achieve it.

Many people think of me as a 'self-made' successful business woman who has created significant wealth from real estate with an annual rental income of half a million pounds; I prefer to describe myself in a different way. Firstly, I do not believe that anybody is 'self'-made. The term implies that a person achieves success alone and arrives at their desired location without any help. My story is far from that – I do not believe that I would be where I am today without the knowledge, help, love and support of many others.

I am who I am because of the life I've lived and the people and things I have been exposed to. Nobody lives in isolation of the world and to label someone as 'self-made' implies success obtained apart from the world, people and their influences.

My background was a humble one. I came to the UK in the mid-1980s as an international student. At the time, like most students from third world countries, you were expected to support yourself. As such, working and studying became a must; not an option. Should you have chosen to have a family, then the multitasking extended from work and study to include raising children.

I juggled a variety of part time jobs in addition to raising a young family and completing a professional Chartered Banker Institute course. It was no easy feat. That period was one of the most challenging times of my life. I was pulled in various directions on a daily basis and had to continuously keep up with the different roles required.

I have learned that with challenge comes the opportunity for growth. A person's life is akin to a muscle; you never know what you are made of or how much you can take until the pressure is on. Some waver and faint under pressure but others see it as an opportune time to strengthen their muscles and build a reserve.

On completing my banking course, none of the banks at the time were willing to offer me employment as I was seen as overqualified! I knew I had to do something and decided to up the ante by casting a wider net, making myself more professionally desirable and completing a Business Finance degree.

So often, people go through life without ever really taking stock to think about what they really want or how they can get it. Things seem easier when we adopt the conventional approach and refuse to go against the grain. We are told to study hard, get a good job and then work harder. If it pays the bills and leaves a surplus of cash at the end of each month to spend as we please then we have 'made it' – albeit by mediocre standards.

Yes, I had a job and a flat but I wasn't satisfied. I disliked the flat, hated the area and loathed the idea of paying rent year in and year out without ever seeing a return or reaching some level of ownership. I felt as though I could achieve more – I knew I could achieve more. I lacked a lot of things; my knowledge was limited and I was going into unknown waters, where entrepreneurship was concerned, but confidence and belief were two things I had in abundance. Once the basics were decided, the next question to tackle was how I'd go about achieving things.

The key components I started with were focus, determination and purpose. I was determined for change to take place and willing to focus for as long as necessary on whatever was required in order to achieve the results I craved. I knew that without purpose, a reason 'why' I wanted change, all my other decisions and commitments would be short lived.

I wanted to create meaningful wealth; money with a mission. I wanted to be financially comfortable and never have the need to 'worry' about money but I also wanted to be a blessing to my family, impact my community and help make a difference globally.

The desire for change propelled me into action but it was my love for people that kept me there. I knew that if I could connect a 'money making' idea to serving people then I was on the right track.

Chapter Two
TAKING ACTION

The first step I took towards achieving change was to go through what I call the five W's – these are foundational questions required to achieve lasting success. Whilst I touch on the five W's in chapter 6, I thoroughly expand on them in my book *'The Five W's of Wealth Creation'*. I had to ask myself difficult questions and search for the answers and solutions.

If my purpose for creating meaningful wealth was really about 'money with a mission', if I really desired 'accumulation for distribution' then the answer to 'why must I create wealth?' would match the purpose. Asking 'why' is a great way of identifying what your real motives and intentions are.

I needed to know:

- Why must I create wealth?

- What kind of wealth do I need to be financially free?

- What does financial freedom look like?

- What kind of wealth do I need to cater for my immediate and extended family?

- What kind of wealth do I need to help support and impact my community?

- What sort of investment do I need to have to help me achieve all of the above?

- What do I currently know?

- What do I need to know?

- Who can I learn from?

- When can I start?

- Where do I start to invest?

There were many other questions I asked myself including all of the questions above and once answered, they led to other questions. But hopefully you have a clear idea of how I laid my foundation.

Before you embark on any endeavour you must count the cost. There are too many incomplete ventures out there and it's always because someone failed to count the cost. I needed to know what achieving the level of success I desired would cost and whether I was willing to pay the price.

Once I had my answers and was satisfied with the fact that I had exhausted all possible solutions I began my second phase which was all about my plan of action.

I must pause for a moment and add something. I was raised in an average home with parents who had little money. I was not an academic genius, nor was I lucky. What I am trying to stress here is the importance of understanding that *success can be achieved by anybody. Even the least likely is a candidate for wealth creation. Wealth and success are choices that are determined by your daily decisions. These 'daily choices' provide the fabric and building blocks for who you become; the choices you make today will determine the opportunities available tomorrow.* There are so many things in this world that are beyond our control. Real change and transformation always begins with 'I' because the only person you a guaranteed to be able to change is you! *Whilst change begins with 'I' it is always achieved with 'we'; true transformation is never completed in isolation.*

I knew that real estate was where I wanted to begin investing. It made the most sense to me based on what I wanted to achieve, my passion and the leverage of using bank money and hands free management. This meant I could achieve my objective with other people's money and time and still have the freedom and flexibility to raise my children.

At the point of making the decision I was living month by month from payslip to payslip. I had to look at creative ways to start saving money. I know many people say they have nothing to save but I disagree. No matter how small it is you can start saving something towards your goal. Uncomfortable – yes possibly, challenging – definitely, impossible – certainly not! If you keep telling yourself you don't have enough money, if you keep saying you have no cash to spare then guess what? That is exactly what you will have. I told myself things like that for many years. All it did was hinder me from starting my wealth creation journey sooner. When it comes to anything in life, perception is always key.

Money *is* available, you just need to see it. I began to take account of all income and expenses. I looked at what I was spending my money on and reviewed areas where I could cut costs. You would be surprised how much difference small changes can make; like taking a packed lunch to work rather than eating out or buying a bus pass for the work commute rather than using the tube.

Respect the pennies and you will see the pounds. Once I was able to create a budget and review my finances it gave me a greater respect for money. I knew that every amount I was able to save, no matter how small, would take me one step closer to realising my goal.

Saving was not the only thing I needed to address. I knew little about real estate and in order to be successful I needed to acquire the relevant knowledge. I began to attend forums and speak to other investors. If there was a seminar, webinar, book, blog or website that could help then I would listen to it, read it and study it. Every single resource that was available and beneficial to me was used. I was a novice and did not shy away from the fact that I needed help. Successful people know that ignorance is okay as long as you do something about it. It will always cost you something whenever and wherever you willingly allow yourself to be ignorant. Even today, after more than 15 years in the industry, I am still learning! It has become a life long journey to continue to intentionally improve and develop.

I researched like-minded individuals. Those who shared the same dream as I did but who are now successful in their own right. I networked and made contact with some of them; all the while keeping abreast of any changes and trends in the real estate world.

In a nutshell; I took action. The opportunities of life are not given to those that are lazy, indecisive and prone to procrastination. They are given to those that take action; those that *do*. The initial two steps I took, contributed towards the start of a coherent and better future.

Property investment is not exclusive to a particular group but anyone who desires to get results in the property market will need to develop specific characteristics and habits. A successful real estate investor must be a person of action. They should be able to plan effectively, organise efficiently and remain goal orientated at all times and in all seasons.

I cannot say that all of these traits came to me naturally but I was able to sharpen the skills I had and develop the one's I needed to get where I desired to be. My journey was not merely a journey of financial freedom; it was a journey of growth, development and discovery – all of which I still actively pursue today.

If money *is* the only thing you are chasing then you are bound to encounter an endless line of unnecessary problems. You are ready to begin your journey of real estate investment when you realise that there is a bigger picture and that bigger picture is more about you than it is about making money. External success and achievement is directly linked to internal success and achievement. By this I mean that you can only produce results that correlate to the person you have become. The two are synonymous.

Chapter Three
WHY PROPERTY?

So why did I choose property? What was so special about having real estate as my investment option?

The answer is threefold:

Firstly, it was instinctive. I wanted financial freedom and I am an advocate for leaving money behind – not debt. I wanted to leave my children, grandchildren and the generations after them with a tangible inheritance. What better way than leaving 'bricks and mortar?'

Secondly, as a young girl growing up in small rented accommodation with my hard working parents, I always admired those successful enough to live in and own spacious, large homes. The experience of raising my eldest child in a cramped, second floor flat without a garden to play in, also served as sizeable motivation for me to delve into property investment.

Thirdly, after much research, I came to the conclusion that in the world where a variety of business models for a multitude of investments exist, property investment met and matched my criteria. It delivered both on the lifestyle I wanted and on my overall objective to create personal and meaningful wealth and help make a difference.

When assessing any potential mode of investment for suitability, make sure that you review the following criteria and ask yourself:

1. Will it benefit me? (short-term/long-term)

2. Will it benefit others? (short-term/long-term)

3. What is the cost and can I afford it? If not, can I get help to fund it?

4. Is it inflation proof?

5. What effort does the initial start-up require?

Benefits – The benefits of real estate supported my objectives and desires. I wanted a solid tangible investment that I could see and touch – something I could leave behind for my family and loved ones. Buy-to-let investment would provide me with rental income I could use to supplement, and eventually replace, my salary. I had the potential to earn the kind of money I could never acquire by working a 9-5 job. The capital growth associated with real estate investment would mean that I could raise capital against the equity in a property, expand my portfolio and buy more properties. If I managed to invest successfully I would soon be able to pay off my residential mortgages as well as any debt. An additional bonus would be the joy of touching lives by providing homes for the homeless and others in need. Those are the main reasons why property investment became such an attractive and appealing option for me.

Cost – Property is costly and you may not have the money to buy outright but someone else may have the funds so money is always available. Whether it be your own or someone else's (OPM – Other People's Money) acquiring cash is usually easier than you think. According to an article in Market Watch [2] the secret to the success of the rich, especially for those in real estate including the likes of Donald Trump, is using other people's money. Bret Arends states that "The fastest and surest way to make money these days is by getting your hands on other people's money — and then putting it to work for you." OPM is essentially money that does not belong to you and is subject to repayment, usually with interest. (e.g. Bank loans, other money lenders, repayable sponsorship, loans from family and friends etc.) Most banks are usually willing to lend against property as security.

Inflation – This criteria is vital to any investment success because the investment becomes a liability if it fails to produce a return above the rate of inflation, especially rising inflation. Rising inflation means that the value of an investment can be eroded over time unless the investment returns have risen above inflation rate. To me, inflation is a slow, silent killer, which gradually diminishes the value of money over time; as well as the value of accumulated savings and investments. It has been proven that property values have risen above inflation; real estate is a great investment at any time and it is even better during times of rising inflation. Limited availability of land and rising population growth will increase housing demand. As a result, real estate in general has the potential to easily beat inflation. In effect, property I bought for £73k in 1998 was independently valued at £325k in 2015.

Start-up effort – I needed to be certain that I could combine property investment with other responsibilities including family commitments and my existing job. At the time, I could not afford to commit to something that would rob me of all my energy and time which were still needed for raising young children and working. The chosen investment needed to fit into my daily routine. Property investment is pliable. You can focus on real estate solely, combine it with something else or have other projects and businesses on the go simultaneously. It was ideal for me as I was able to pursue other things whilst building on my property portfolio.

Property type – As a potential property investor, the type of property you should look for depends on your goals and strategy. Your property type or types should always be determined by what you are trying to achieve. For example, if a new investor decides to invest in a large three-storey-high house with multiple occupation (i.e. rented out by at least five people who are not from one 'household' (a family) but share facilities like the bathroom and kitchen) then mandatory licences and time allocation for the management of all the individual occupants will be required. Although it yields more rental income and cash flow, it also demands much more maintenance. Some investors relish and thrive on this type of challenge, but you must have the time and effort required to make it a success.

Purely due to the high demand, I prefer single family tenancy of 2 to 3 bed houses. Larger properties sometimes take longer to let, demand is often minimal and interest can be lukewarm. As a rule of thumb, I opt for residential properties rather than commercial. But that is not to say that if I see a good opportunity in the commercial sector I won't jump at it. When I was starting out in real estate, the residential sector proved to be an easier option than the commercial sector. The thought of providing a roof over someone else's head motivates me. In addition, banks and other lenders have strict criteria with higher costs/fees where lending for commercial purposes are concerned. Another point to consider is that as the economy went into recession, high street businesses were hit hard with an increase in online businesses. As a result, a sizeable number of high street shops in the commercial sector were forced to close. By contrast, the residential sector thrived; a shortage of homes increased rental prices for residential property.

For the new property investor who chooses to focus on buy-to-let property there are four key process to success which I call the 'Fantastic Four':

1. **Find** – Finding a property to buy for investment

2. **Fund** – Financing the cost of the property must be considered. Before you let the property, be sure to include not just the purchase cost, but also furnishing costs as well as 2 to 3 months rental into your calculations – taking into consideration possible void periods when the property may be empty. You must also consider various outgoing costs including maintenance, insurance and other required work.

3. **Furnish** – Furnish the property adequately to help you achieve the best return on your investment – it will also aid in appealing to renters. Make sure the property adheres to all regulations before it is occupied with tenants.

4. **Fill/Flip** – This stage is where you put your strategy into motion be it for renting or flipping and you choose to either let the property or sell it.

Chapter Four

BUYING PROPERTY

At every phase of the investment process you must be able to use the necessary keys to unlock each opportunity.

When buying property an investor must answer the following 'W' questions:

- What price am I paying for the property?

- Where have I purchased the property? (Where is it located with regards to rental demand?)

- What finances will I require?

What price am I paying for the property?

The amount you pay for the property determines how much you make when selling or refinancing for capital growth profit.

You must always find and purchase property below the market value (BMV) as you only make money when you buy. This proves true even in the seller's market. Try to negotiate a minimum of a 15% reduction or look for property that is undervalued by 15% or more, even if it requires light renovation. Remember any discount is better than no discount at all.

Where have I purchased the property?

Buying property where people would like to live and in a promising area that is going through regeneration will result in high rental demand. It should be an area that has local amenities and is still below the UK average market price. These areas can be hard to find but they are out there; they are sleeping giants – waiting to be woken. In the early part of the year 2000, I started investing in Dagenham as it was affordable and fit within my expected yield. There were proposed investments for both the roads and railway services. House values in the area have more than doubled in the last 10 years.

With buy-to-let properties, aim for purchases with a yield of 8% and above. You must ensure the rental rate covers the mortgage and all expenses with extra cash as a buffer every month.

Buy property for rental income not just capital growth as the latter is buying based on prediction and no one can fully predict property prices.

What finances will I require?

Finance is essential. Try to finance your investments with savings, low interest loans or through friends and family. Always look for finance that does not have negative long term implications and be prepared to wait. It's better to take the time to get the necessary funds together rather than speedball into a messy financial agreement that could have negative consequences.

The types of financial products you acquire should be linked to your strategy. For example, if you are trying to grow your portfolio (with a mortgage), you must look for financial products that have no penalty in repaying the amount borrowed when you decide to move your mortgage to another lender or increase your borrowing or even pay the mortgage off.

Furnish your property. When furnishing or decorating a property you have purchased, especially below market value, you must try and add value to the property. The main areas of focus that will yield the greatest return are the kitchen, bathroom and modernisation and layout changes. They can all add value and appeal to would-be-renters. The right improvements made in the right places can easily increase value. An increase in value will enable you to take out your existing capital outlay for further purchases.

When preparing to let consider decorating and furnishing the property to a good or high standard that is suitable to your tenant type – not your own taste. Paint walls in neutral colours. Magnolia with a gloss finish, as opposed to vibrantly bright or dark colours, may be bland but it is clean, fresh and easy to work with when it comes to colour schemes and matching furniture. Ensure kitchen units and bathrooms are fitted to correct standards with reputable contractors. Replacing knackered kitchen units or an outdated bathroom can be advantageous as it can enhance the property as well as count towards revenue expenses, which can be applied towards your profit.

Fill your property. When buying-to-let you must aim to fill your property as soon as possible. An empty house is a costly one. My void periods are usually a maximum of 5 days between lets. The shorter the void period then the less time wasted losing potential income from occupancy.

The future of property

There is a great deal that can be said when it comes to property investment and it is impossible to cover everything in a short chapter such as this. I have simply tried to provide an overview and hone in on some key points that are essential to those staring out.

The core message is you must know from the onset what you are trying to achieve; income, capital growth or both? Your strategy will determine what type of property you need and how much you are willing to pay for it; this will determine where you look (location) and cap how much you spend.

The Bank of England base rate has been at its lowest for some time now and borrowing has become cheaper as result. Although not set in stone, my view is that interest rates will rise slowly between late 2016 and 2017.

According to land registry figures from 2014, house prices rose in England and Wales by 7% - with London seeing a rise of 16.3%. Therefore, I believe buy-to-let landlords, especially those that want to expand their portfolio, need to review existing portfolios to see if there is available equity that can be taken from their property. Property investors should also make a decision on whether they wish to re-mortgage using the equity in their existing portfolio to add value, increase portfolio size or pay off mortgages with more than a 75% loan to the property value.

My advice in light of recent changes, especially for private investor portfolio landlords with higher mortgages or residential ones, would be to try and reduce the mortgage significantly or pay it off completely depending on personal goals. My plan is to increase my portfolio, within a limited company, in areas that are yet to catch up with the average UK house price. I have re-mortgaged some properties (with a large equity) to finance the new purchases in my limited company and used some extra cash raised for opportune deals as cash is king!

Top tips for those who desire to re-mortgage:

- Review the existing product you have to ensure there are no redemption penalties. Work out your exit and legal fees, total the costs and then compare them to the cost of a new deal.

- Contact your existing lender to see whether they offer product transfers as this may save you fees on brokers and may help your credit file etc.

- Look for whole market brokers, with no ties to any one lender, who can help work out the best deal for you and your circumstances.

The July 2015 Budget saw several key changes that will impact landlords. In particular was the restriction on mortgage interest relief and the autumn review of higher stamp duty charges for buy-to-let. Landlords should not panic. Firstly, the change does not affect corporate landlords who invest using a company. Secondly, the changes will not fully come into play until 2017 so there is still time to plan ahead, develop and apply the correct strategies in order to achieve your objectives.

All landlords will fall into one of three categories:

1. Landlords who are basic rate tax payers (those with small portfolios that fall under the basic tax bracket will not be affected).

2. Landlords who will become higher rate tax payers as a result of the changes (the tax bracket move is due to the changes and may impact the majority of landlords).

3. Landlords who are currently higher rate tax payers.

If you are currently a high rate tax payer or will fall into the high rate tax bracket, due to other income, my advice would be to start reviewing your portfolio. The options available to you depend on your individual circumstances and your strategy.

Some possible options are:

1. Pay off or reduce high interest mortgages.

2. Sell off properties with high interest.

3. Re-mortgage high interest properties to a lower interest rate.

4. Transfer existing property into a company (you have to bear in mind the CGT and SDT; also withdrawing from a company can be expensive).

5. Transfer ownership to a partner who is a basic tax payer (you have to consider tax liabilities especially as values may have increased).

6. Landlords with other jobs may consider reducing hours or quitting if income shoots above the basic rate.

7. Give! Charity contributions or even increased pension contributions could help.

8. Use the wear and tear allowance as an opportunity to complete repairs.

Available options will depend on individual circumstances and I advise all landlords to speak to their accountant or seek financial advice and obtain professional counsel.

There are a considerable amount of things to consider when it comes to purchasing property. Hopefully I have given you a taster of what to expect and provided a starting point of areas for consideration.

Chapter Five
A SUCCESSFUL PROPERTY MAGNATE

Most landlords, especially the accidental landlord, think about profit only and do not consider the other elements. For any beginner or would-be investor there are fundamental questions that must be answered in order to make a success; I call them the five W's of property investment. Every investor must take the time to answer these questions before proceeding to invest in buy-to-let property.

Key questions – the five W's

Why property?

Answering this will motivate you – especially when you hit the harsh realities of property investment. Your 'why' will ensure you carry on and keep going until you reach your goal. If your why is not strong enough, any changes in legislation may throw you off course and you will never reach your destination of building wealth through real estate. Are you investing to supplement your income? Do you desire to fund your pension and retirement using the rental income or capital growth? Are you hoping to leave a legacy for your family? Would you like to fund a project close to your heart and help your community? Discover *your* answer 'why' and lay the foundation for your success.

Who will guide you through?

This question is all about who you can learn from. You must identify the right mentors, experts and information that will help you achieve your goal in good time, with little stress, minimal risk and maximum profit.

You should also include the team of professionals you will need to work or affiliate with in the 'who' section (e.g. contractors, solicitors, estate agents, accountants, independent surveyor etc.)

According to KPMG's recent survey of 200 female entrepreneurs, including 5000 companies, finding a mentor to guide you through was the second essential key to successful business [3].

What are your goals and objectives?

The 'what' questions are linked to your 'why' answers. You must assess things like required finances and availability of time. For new buy-to-let investors with less experience and investors who have less time to manage properties, single let properties managed by reputable agents are ideal compared to HMO (Houses in Multiple Occupation) which require more time and expertise. What type of property you invest in depends on your goal. If your goal is high cash flow from rental income and you have the time and expertise to manage the properties then HMO could be ideal. Property type will also determine the type of tenant you wish to rent to. If your target tenant is family then single let may be ideal.

Different types of property produce different yields. Whilst there are exceptions, generally HMO's usually produce a higher yield but require specific expertise as discussed above. Terraced houses usually meet the needs of families and flats are normally preferred by professionals.

Where?

Location is key; *buy a great property in the wrong location and it could prove detrimental.*

Always buy near good roads, transport links, amenities and good schools. If you can cover all or most of the above then you widen your scope for tenant type. If you desire to be a hands-on landlord then you should think about purchasing property near you. Most landlords I know invest near where they live as they know the area well and don't want to travel too far because they are the ones managing the property. If you are an investor who has limited time, then feel free to go further afield - as long as you have a reputable agent within your target location. If you cannot afford the area you live in or if the rental market near you is unfavourable then take courage and venture out. You will be surprised at the opportunities available once you start looking.

Search for an area close to where there are major redevelopment projects in transport links and infrastructure. I call these areas *sleeping giants* as their prices tend to rise higher than other areas. Locations with new retail parks can also be good stimulators for increased demand in housing.

If you want to target student tenants, then your property must be near a university and you must be prepared for high turnover in comparison to single family lets who usually stay for a longer period and take better care of the property.

When?

Your 'when' is all about identifying the right time to buy. Timing is important. Establishing the right time is all about having the other components in place first. Things like understanding why you are investing in property, what your goals are, what's required to achieve them, obtaining the right knowledge and know-how, sourcing a good team etc. are all key to the right timing.

If you are targeting a sleeping giant or bordering the expensive areas then the timing can be critical.

Real estate success can be identified by three categories, known as the three P's. Each 'P' has essential points to consider in order to achieve success.

1) The _Person_ investing must be

Motivated

Determined

Tenacious

2) The _Property_ itself

Price paid must be below market value

Location of property must have a high rental demand

Property type must match your strategy (e.g. mid-terraced/HMO)

Market type must be established (family let/student/professional/DSS)

3) The _Profit_ (benefits)

Property capital growth

Rental income derived

Most investors consider only the profit, i.e. the benefit; this tends to contribute to their failure long term. All P's must be considered to achieve long term success.

I spend a considerable amount of my time mentoring and advising people that desire to go into property investment and many of the same topics repeatedly come up as points of discussion. Answering the five W's and using the three P's as category guidelines will provide you with the necessary key elements and processes required for any successful property investor.

Chapter Six

BUYING PROPERTY ABROAD

Buying property locally or in a particular country is not the only thing that must be thought about. Where you buy property is also key as making a success in property investment is not fixed to a particular country. You must go where you can achieve maximum success. Having said that, you need the know-how and should be aware of the pitfalls that lie in investing abroad; this will help you – when deciding whether you wish to purchase property in other countries.

I am a great believer in capitalising on opportunities and I do not limit them to the ones on my doorstep but will go wherever a favourable chance presents itself; as long as I am able to build reliable and professional contacts who can verify the market and manage things in my absence. You must always leverage on time and *OPK (Other People's Knowledge)*.

If you decide to invest overseas, my advice is to ensure your investments make a profit and meet your original objectives. A budding investor must:

- Source a trustworthy agent who can source or manage the property for you.

- Have reliable professional contacts on the ground - including solicitors, contractors etc.

- Implement the necessary infrastructure to deal with possible language and culture differences.

- Understand all related barriers - as well as ways to manage them effectively.

- Understand laws relating to landlords and real estate management in the country

Investors must complete their own due diligence and gain understanding of the legal responsibilities for their country of choice, as well as keep up to date with changes in all matters relating to investors of real estate, including tax legislation and management responsibilities. Things vary from country to country and you must be clear on what your responsibilities are as an investor and what you are liable for. Even the smallest oversight could be detrimental. You will need to factor in all extra costs and fees including accountant /management fees, taxes, etc.

In 2007 I made an investment in Dubai. During that time a foreigner could purchase property, most of which were new builds, and pay for it in instalments. I decided to make the investment only after addressing the points raised above and thoroughly completing due diligence.

I also considered the following:

1. The likely rental yield – after deducting service charges
2. The location
3. The reputation of the contractors and building companies
4. The level of demand for similar properties in the area
5. The eviction process – in the event that tenants failed to make payment
6. Known or possible risks versus known or possible gains

I ensured I travelled to Dubai to see, first-hand, how the system worked. I discovered it was normal practice for a year's rent to be paid in advance, which was a pleasant surprise. I decided to take the risk and bought the property (an apartment I could afford). It was one of the best investments I have ever made.

If you have a desire to invest abroad then you must conduct in-depth research and obtain expert or specialist guidance where necessary. The success of an overseas investment hinges on your ability to research beforehand, as poor research may result in considerable loss.

A word of warning to the potential investor: proceed with caution and tread very carefully. A wrong decision could be damaging. You should be mindful and take care to avoid or be extra vigilant of countries where there is a lack of accountability or the presence of regulating bodies. If there is no means of monitoring or accreditation, you and your money, may end up in the hands of the unscrupulous and bogus.

Experience has taught me that it is always a better option to first travel to the country you intend to invest in and observe how things work in the areas you intend to target for investment, irrespective of whether or not you have a reputable agent.

Buying abroad can be lucrative and the rewards can be bountiful but you must know what you are doing. ***Do not rush into all invitations to purchase abroad without due diligence*** and remember conducting due diligence does not happen overnight. If you can exercise patience and purchase property within the correct safeguards then it could prove to be profitable and worthwhile.

Chapter Seven

LESSONS LEARNED

During the late 1980s I had a small amount of savings. Together with credit card cheques, I was able to make a deposit on my first property; a 2 bedroom house in Plaistow, East London. I immediately let out the property to a long-term tenant whilst I continued to live in my rented flat.

By the early 90s interest rates had climbed to 15%. Unfortunately, they did not stop there and continued to rise steadily. Due to my inexperience, I had made my first major mistake and did not make an allowance for any problems or challenges that may occur – including a rise in interest. I had no back-up plan. To add to my woes, my tenant stopped paying rent. I was left with no choice but to hand the keys to my first 2 bedroom house back to the lender.

I had learnt a vital lesson the hard way. I discovered what damaging pitfalls lay ahead when I failed to plan properly or allow for a contingency.

As a result, I was introduced to the 'ugly' side of investment. *If you have all the opportunity in the world fall at your feet but fail to plan, count the cost and <u>then</u> take action, the opportunities will be wasted.* At the time, everything looked good. It seemed as though I was finally starting to take the large and necessary strides towards fulfilling my dreams; but it was short-lived.

I knew I was destined to create wealth through real estate, my 'why' answers kept pushing me to start again; so with that in mind, I refused to accept defeat. When unforeseen challenges trip us up we are always faced with two options. We either fall and stay down or we get up and keep going. I knew I had to pick myself up, dust myself down and try again. I was not going to accept defeat, on the contrary, I became even more motivated to achieve success in real estate. I decided to create a plan B and put it into action.

Mistakes are inevitable and we all experience failure to one degree or another. The tragedy is when we fail to stop, take stock and learn from our mishaps. Errors can cost but the lessons, if learned, have the potential to be priceless.

I have not always got it right. My first property purchase, as mentioned, is a prime example. Things can go wrong so don't be hard on yourself if they do – especially if you are completely new to property investment. Assess what went wrong, how it went wrong and then begin to look at ways you can resolve the issue or develop strategies on how to avoid it happening again.

I also had a negative experience investing in the United States of America a few years ago. I had done my research and asked the relevant questions, conducted an investigation into the legal aspects and the landlord's responsibilities. However, I made a fundamental error and relied heavily on information provided by agents who later went into administration (for unrelated business) and the contracts provided turned out to be fraught with holes. Whilst it is impossible to control other peoples' actions I should have conducted more research independently and not relied heavily on the agent's word.

I had used reputable agents in the UK whom I trusted and I believed their marketing materials and testimonials. I assumed the changes in the referral overseas would be monitored as the American agents had a good track record in the UK.

I was not informed early enough once the American agents, who were supposed to be managing my portfolio, went bankrupt. I was left with a portfolio that had little to no rental income. The agents kept changing hands along with the portfolio and disputes arose about the authenticity of repair charges, inflated repair quotes and other additional costs. I was unable to challenge cost queries at opportune times as I was not residing in the country and the problems mounted as they were not immediately addressed. The alleged cost of repairs and the like, ensured that any rental income that was due was never paid.

I also made investment errors by investing in off plan property (these are properties sold before the structure has been constructed) in Auckland New Zealand, St Lucia and Las Vegas. All of which never materialised. Dates kept being postponed and then the recession kicked in.

Although I believe my error of relying on the developer was partly to be blame, the main failure of these particular investments was largely due to a downturn in the economy. As a result of the general economic decline, banks began to withdraw their finances from committed building projects. Demand for property slumped and building projects that were scheduled for completion in two years stretched to four years and beyond, with builders requesting more and more capital from investors; yet there was no guarantee that once completed, the properties could be sold or let. Needless to say, it was a complete disaster and I lost approximately £250,000.

At the time, a quarter of a million pounds was a significant amount of money for me to lose. I was shaken to the core by the loss; but I managed to pick myself up. I was determined not to let the setback drag me down and wanted it to serve as motivation for me to get back out there and recover the loss. *In times of crisis you always have a choice; you can either let the crisis rule you or you can take over the crisis!* I chose to use the temporary setback as an opportunity to create change and introduced systems and infrastructures that would facilitate a better outcome for future projects.

So how did I do it? It was nothing fancy or extravagant. I simply went back to basics and did what I do best; I asked myself some honest and difficult questions:

1. What happened exactly?
2. Why and where did I go wrong?
3. Was it self-inflicted?
4. Who or what was to blame?
5. Did I plunge into the investments in haste and without thoroughly checking the facts?
6. Did I overlook something important?

Although there were a few reasons which were beyond my control, I accepted that I was partly to blame for not paying enough attention and heeding to the warning signs. I took responsibility. The downturn in the economy exacerbated an already difficult situation and if I had been more attentive, I would have realised that one of the companies I was dealing with was about to close down as a result of staff members embezzling capital.

I decided to take stock of what remained from that particular investment and was able to strengthen it through what I call a damage limitation exercise. I did not dwell too much on the loss and decided to move on firmly putting it behind me but having learned the hard way, how not to invest in uncompleted overseas projects. Are off plan projects bad investments? No. Are overseas off plan projects bad investments? No. I simply didn't complete the necessary due diligence required and missed the warning signs as a result of my poor assessments.

There is a clear difference between 'knowing' and 'doing'. I *knew* the right things to do but failed to actually do them and it cost me. When an opportunity comes our way we are usually eager to grab it with both hands, especially if it's something that has worked in the past.

My advice, in any major crisis is this; take absolute responsibility. Only then will you be able to get up and start again. If you blame someone else, even if they are at fault, you may spend a lifetime waiting for them to acknowledge accountability and make amends. When you reach a place where you are able to stand up and say "I take full responsibility for my failures" then you can begin to move forward.

I liken it to a jogger who suddenly trips on something while out running. He cannot stay in a place of injury; he has to move on! *If you can move forward when hurt or injured, then the investment world becomes a much easier place once you are at optimum health.*

Whatever the mistake or error was; review the situation, learn from it, accept responsibility and have a positive attitude so that you can get back on track, stronger than you were before.

Chapter Eight

MAKE MONEY, NOT EXCUSES

At the start of my journey even though I was working fulltime, raising a family, renting a small flat and had very little income, I was very ambitious. I did not let my current circumstances stop me following my dreams and proceeding with my plan.

I was a working class lone mother. With my partner working overseas, I had to juggle work with raising four children. I had every reason to make a valid excuse and not step out, but I decided that anything worth any value would require my time, energy and commitment. I wanted more for my life and the life of my family and so I knew I had to change, grow and develop to go further than I ever had.

After losing my first house I began to think about alternative ways to make money. I was living in a three bedroom flat on the third floor in an estate block, but I had an extra room which I was able to sublet.

I took on a part time cleaning job, set myself a savings target and an achievement timescale. Then I set about learning the practicalities of global financial investments. I looked at how various investments worked to deliver, not just in terms of supplement income, but as instruments of wealth creation.

All of the hard work paid off. Once backed with my savings, coupled with opportunities to use **OPM** (Other People's Money i.e. a small overdraft cheque) and armed with knowledge of the property investment world, I was able to start again in early 2000, with a deposit of £5000 (the £5000 came from savings and a bank overdraft). I paid a 10% deposit on a £50,000 property. Aided by the now benign economic climate, I sold the property at £65,000 and used the profit to make a deposit for my family home. I also used the balance as deposit for a buy-to-let property. I was not averse to taking risks and calculated that I could re-mortgage the house and use the additional funds raised to fund more properties without significant financial detriment.

This simple yet effective formula set me on my way and subsequently, I began the process of establishing myself as a major player and wealth creator globally, in the property investment field. *APPA* is what I have coined my formula for success. It simply means:

- Ask the right questions
- Plan
- Prepare
- Act

Everyone has the ability within them to create wealth. I call this ability to create a *seed of greatness*. The seed of greatness is a seed that enables you to grow your own money tree. The seed is not exclusive, it resides in every individual and without planting it wealth cannot be created.

Your seed of greatness will not initially come in the form of money. The capital layout for your venture may translate as your skills and natural talent, it may even be mentorship through a key relationship. Some people get uncomfortable at the concept of 'selling' themselves, figuratively speaking, but the truth of the matter is that life is made up of a continual pool of exchange. It is a process of giving and receiving, sowing and reaping. You will only ever receive to the proportion that you are willing to give or put in. Nothing just happens in business. Success comes as a result of like-for-like intentional input and a sequence of deliberate choices.

Look at it this way; if a farmer wanted a mango tree then he would plant mango seed. If someone said they were planting apple seeds because they wanted mangos, you would label them ludicrous. Yet that is what people do in the world of business on a daily basis. They want to make millions yet their input is minimal; they have the character, worth ethic and attitude of a lazy person with no aspirations. They give as little as they can possibly get away with and the outcome is never what they desire.

Planning: You must plan. Everybody has ideas but the majority do nothing with them. Ideas only become beneficial when they are ignited and initiated through planning.

A farmer who decides he wants to create wealth by selling oranges, has to make a clear decision from the outset that that he is not just going to produce and sell oranges for his own consumption. In order to create wealth he knows that he must be able to produce and sell enough to create significant income from it. Once this is established, he needs to think about how to make it happen. He will begin to consider factors like the size of the land, the right type of equipment, when to start sowing and what help will be required. The farmer will seek out the necessary resources and building blocks that produce his harvest, building towards a successful future.

Preparation: This phase is where you reinforce the foundations laid down during the planning stage. What you do here, if done correctly, will help you launch the implementation or action stage.

Action: Taking action is one of those things that sounds easier in theory than in practice. This phase is where all of your planning and preparatory work come into play. If you have failed to plan and prepare then it will be evidenced at this stage. The action period should be the most rewarding because it is the doing, the implementation. It is where you begin to see the fruits of your labour.

A note of caution to the potential investor; it is important to get the sequence of events right. It could be financially disadvantageous to act when you really should be planning. Successful property investors do not buy and let properties *before* working out what the yield will be. It is a recipe for failure: so make sure you plan, prepare then act.

If you desire to go into real estate investment timing is important; the sensitivity of accurate timing applies to most investments but is especially important in property investment. As long as you get the timing right, you can profit in property. The key to timing is this: in a buyers' market you buy and in a sellers' market – if you have to sell property that has appreciated in value then sell or refinance and raise funds on a property with great equity. It all depends on what you are trying to achieve. You may wish to pay off some debt or retire or increase your portfolio. Sounds simple enough but you'd be surprised at the number of people that try desperately to buy, especially in an area that is overpriced with little yield, when they should be selling. They end up paying over the odds.

If opting to invest with OPM, then the right time is when interest rates are low. You should also ensure that the amount borrowed is substantial enough to hold some in reserve, so that you can manage unexpected issues as they arise.

Having one portfolio will not necessarily create immediate wealth, but having several – spread over various property types usually stands a budding investor in good stead to start creating wealth.

We all have the potential to create the wealth we desire but a lot of people often allow a variety of excuses to get in the way. They find a problem with family, age, current income and savings, debt, work commitments, lack of information or time. The list is in actual fact a lot longer as the reasons are quite vast and can vary from person to person.

In all instances excuses, like those listed above, are used to justify a lack of creativity, drive and passion. It is easier to fear and err on the side of caution than to dream big. People rarely look for opportunities to multiply what little resources they have even if it is made available to them.

What about debt?

(By 'debt' I mean if you are in debt on non-essentials, and you need to move on to invest in property by first clearing the debt and starting to save in order to invest).

In terms of accruing debt, whilst there are noble reasons that do not stem from a place of self-indulgence, for the majority the cause is usually less honourable. People are simply living beyond their means. Many will react strongly to that sentence and be the first to try and refute it. They will show you their outgoings and explain how their income always leaves them short. Delve a little deeper and you will find the cash spent on takeaways, non-essential clothing and cosmetics, nights out etc. It's not that any of these things are wrong – it's just that the western culture has bought into a lie that implies the essentials and bare necessities encompass things we do not actually need.

There are those who do not want to deny themselves all the gadgets that 21st century technology has to offer. They want to live the dream without first acquiring the building blocks that will make their dream a reality and sustain it. They want to eat lobster on a sardine budget. As a result, they are always spending tomorrow's cash today.

If you are in debt you must be completely honest with yourself about why you are where you are. If it's due to poor decisions and a lack of self-control then admit it!

Before you purchase anything you should always ask:

1. Do I really need this?

2. Do I really need this now?

3. Can I afford it?

Ask yourself:

1. Why am I struggling financially?

2. Why am I in debt?

3. What do I need to do in order to get out of debt?

If you are currently in debt do not fret, change is possible. Your future does not have to be one of doom and gloom. I always say to people, if there is a reverse gear then there is also a forward gear. At different stages and in different seasons we all want to run when we should be walking or even crawling. There is a process and order to everything created; just like a baby who first learns how to sit, crawl, stand and then walk. *An accumulation of debt means you have probably skipped a step or two in the process.*

You may have spent more than you earn for a period of time which then had a ripple effect on all of your finances. You may have had an unexpected expense or experienced a period where you received no income or were required to fund something such as a funeral – or financially support a family member or loved one.

For some, debt may have built up over a number of years. Be patient; if it took years to get into that level of debt then it will take time to get out of it. A plan of action is required. The first thing you must do is *spend less than you earn*. Below are some practical steps to ensure you can reduce your expenses:

• Take stock of all your income and expenses. Record to the very penny what comes in and what goes out. From those records you must derive your priority needs. Things you desire are not necessarily priorities. An inability to say 'no' or 'not right now' to your children on non-essential items does not equate to a priority either. Your priorities should include things like your rent/mortgage, utility bills, transportation (for work purposes), food, essential clothing, giving to charities and those less well-off and tithes and offerings (if you are a Christian).

- Cut expenses. This stage is not negotiable and any expense that isn't a priority should be removed or reduced. Name-brands aren't always the best value or quality. Make do without the luxury items and stick to essential needs only.

- Create a list of all your debts and place them in order of priority with the high interest debts at the top. Assess your repayment plans and ask yourself which debts can be reduced first.

- Cultivate the habit of saving money even while you are adjusting to a more austere lifestyle. Try and have automatic deductions made from your earnings, no matter how small. Don't sign up to a gym - exercise at home; take a packed lunch to work instead of buying expensive sandwiches; grocery shop online as it's easier to stick to a budget; cook meals at home rather than order takeaway etc. The list of ideas is exhaustive, you just need to get creative.

- Learn the mechanics of money; recognise money is only a means of exchange. It is a tool that can be used successfully or poorly. Discover how to increase it, grow it, manage it and monitor it.

- Cultivate the habit of giving (my philosophy is you do not reap where you have not sown; if you give you will receive).

It's easier to be intentional about saving when you save for a purpose and not just for rainy days. You must think about your future; think about when you reach the season of life where you have aged and are unable to work.

No matter your current situation; whether in debt or debt free, single or married, unemployed, working one job or several – you still have the option to work towards success and begin to create wealth. Obstacles are a part of life, if you allow them to become excuses then you will never achieve to your full potential. Making lots of purposeful money is possible – you just need to believe it.

Chapter Nine

RIGHT MIND-SET

At the beginning of this book I asked you a question about how you see the world. Your perception of a thing will always provide great insight into your mind-set. It is possible to have all of the components for wealth creation and still fail because your mind-set doesn't match. Both what you think and how you think are key.

If you can begin with addressing your qualities and developing them where necessary, then you can begin to forge disciplines that become habits and will eventually be grafted into the way you think and alter your mind-set for the better.

Before I could get out of my flat and become a property investor, I had to act like one; before I could act like one, I had to think like one; and before I could think like one, I had to discover what the make-up of a successful property investor looked like.

I have listed some critical qualities needed to achieve success in property investment below:

- **Goal Setting:** Having a goal before stepping out into the real estate world is essential. *Creating wealth is a journey* and it is an unwise thing to set out on a journey without knowing where you are going. If you don't have a goal and strategy in place, you can be easily distracted and quickly drawn into all sorts of schemes. There are ways to invest in property. For example, single let/HMO/rent-to-rent scheme for those who don't have immediate funds for a deposit to buy a property etc.

  I invest in single lets and enjoy agents managing my properties as I want to concentrate on investment rather than working for income. I like traditional family home single let properties as they are simple, steady and meet my requirements. HMO and rent-to-rent schemes are two other alternatives that may to be suitable for people who have the time and expertise required. Rent-to-rent is a good alternative for people who have time but little finance, it's a way of making money in real estate without actually owning property or needing a mortgage. You simply rent other people's properties and make money from the difference.

- **Learning:** *If you learn more you can earn more.* It would be ignorant of anyone to think that they know everything; learning is a lifelong process. You must be able to learn from others who have been where you want to go. Read the relevant books, purchase the necessary material, attend suitable seminars, join applicable forums and consider having a mentor. As the market changes; you must change. Grow with the times and don't allow yourself to be left behind. Forward thinking, intentional growth through learning and an increase in applicable knowledge and understanding will ensure you keep up and stay ahead where it counts.

- **Organisation:** Organisational skills are essential because you will have legal responsibilities and must be able to keep on top of them all. Failure to keep track of statutory requirements like regulations, certifications, licensing and accurate record keeping could lead to fines and penalties. Keeping abreast of changes in the law is also important because there are legal implications for omitting responsibilities. Running foul of the law is the last thing an investor needs when starting up.

  Ignorance can be costly. Mandatory property licences for landlords was recently introduced by a London Borough Council and a number of landlords were not even aware of its implementation until it was too late. They faced penalties of up to £20,000. Good organisation means good planning and good administration; it will ensure avoidance of such mishaps. A good way to keep up to date with changes as well as receive relevant updates in laws affecting property is to join a landlord association or forum.

- **Management:** You will, more than likely, need to oversee anything of significance. Money, time and relationships all need to be effectively managed. It is not just about making money but keeping money in reserve available for reinvestment. It is crucial for an investor to have some reserve and not spend the profit from rental income on perishable items as this will almost definitely create problems when funds are needed to resolve emergencies such as roof leaks, burst pipes, boiler breakdowns etc.

  A significant number of landlords I have met with 4 or 5 properties, routinely go on expensive holidays, buy brand new luxury cars, live in expensive homes and spend most of their rental income rather than keeping some in reserve for emergencies or reinvestment. Subsequently, in times of emergency, they begin looking for loans to cover shortfalls that are of their own making. This lack of responsibility does not make a successful property investor.

- **Communication:** Communication is key when it comes to managing tenants and contractors. Any budding property investor must be articulate, friendly and good at rapport building. However, that must be tempered with assertiveness and the ability to remain firm, fair and professional at all times, as well as having the ability to negotiate. If you look after your own property then the key to coherently managing your tenants is communication.

  Investors who feel that being able to deal with people, such as agents, contractors and tenants – and communicate with them effectively or in a tactful manner is not their forte, may end up losing potential clients and representatives. Real estate investment is a field that requires good people skills.

The qualities of a successful entrepreneur are the same for anyone desiring to create wealth through real estate. They include:

- Having the mind-set of an investor and creating winning ideas at any cost. Some people call it right or positive attitude. This means you become forward looking, searching for solutions in times of crisis instead of playing the blame game. It also means having confidence and courage to endure pain and criticism.

- Setting purposeful and powerful targets that move you and propel you to action. Purposeful goals will motivate you and give you a sense of achievement.

- Good administration - every good thing is God-given and must be administered effectively if it is to last and grow.

- Successfully developing a work and life balance. You must ensure you have a balanced life otherwise you will burnout and lose control. Successful people live disciplined lives, they know what to prioritise and what to place on the backburner.

The qualities listed are not merely a check list – they are guides that highlight what and how you should be thinking. If you have the right mind-set then your actions and decisions will follow suit.

Remember – success begins with how you think!

Chapter Ten

WEALTH CREATION

Wealth is visible fruit that is always produced by seed. Wealth creation requires seed from its creator, either in the form of abilities, skills, opportunities, time, knowledge or action. You must contribute something towards your future to create the wealth you desire. If you believe that wealth creation is about getting all you can and canning all you get then you are sorely mistaken. *Saving money and hoarding all that comes your way will not produce lasting wealth.* You cannot pray yourself to wealth creation, you must do something; it requires action and it is the action that plants the seed and releases the principle of sowing and reaping.

The biblical story of the widow of Zarephath [4] is an excellent analogy.

A jar of oil and one last meal was all the widow had left in the world when Elijah, the prophet, came to her and asked for some water and bread. The widow of Zarephath sowed her 'seed', she gave out of all that she had. The result was that the jar of oil and the meal she had would not run out and she would be able to feed herself and her child for many days to come.

The story reminds me that we must not be afraid to use what we have no matter how little. An act of faith can result in multiplication of even the smallest thing. Sow and invest your gifts, talents, money, time and opportunities that you have available to you. The widow recognised that Elijah could help her, likewise you must identify those who can help you.

There was another widow in the Bible who had nothing except a jar of oil [5]. That was enough to start her journey out of debt as she followed the instructions given to her.

Both stories highlight the fact that things are never as bleak as they seem. If you can remain hopeful then there is always a way out, there is always something that can be done to bring about change.

You can still give something back even if it's not money. You can give your time to help someone, provide advice on the steps you took to achieve your success and the lessons you learned. *We all have something to give.* I have seen people who have given their time to help others and tremendously increased as a result of it.

There is a true story about a lady who came to the UK but did not have the correct employment papers. As a result she was voluntarily cleaning for the elderly and those with disabilities. She did not ask people for money, she just wanted to help. An old and disabled woman took such a liking to the lady that her family asked that the lady move into their home and help look after the old woman. She did this gladly and was the primary helper until the old woman passed away. When the old woman's will was read, the lady discovered that she had been included and left a significant amount of money. There was no motive or agenda, she had simply decided to help – giving of her time and services to someone in need and she was greatly rewarded for it.

True success always leaves a trail. For those budding investors and entrepreneurs out there who would like to become wealth creators and benefit from further advice remember that the art of wealth creation is not just about what you do; *it is equally about who you become.* As you delve into the property investment world make sure you do it with both feet forward and both eyes open. Give it your all and you are sure to reap a harvest that perpetuates the fruitful production of wealth creation again and again and again.

Becoming a great property investor is a journey that can be taken by anyone willing to walk through the necessary steps. Successful real estate investment is not achieved through pot luck; the results are obtained deliberately by those who have identified the necessary keys and followed the right steps. You can become a successful property magnate if you wish. Make the decision, apply the required keys and take the first steps. There is more than enough room for you in the world of property – so get started and jump in; your path to successful investment awaits you!

ABOUT THE AUTHOR

Elizabeth Benjamin is a business woman, author and mentor with a passion for finance and people. Having worked over 14 years for the local authority in housing, Elizabeth started her wealth creation journey with just £5k and a burning desire to discover a successful path to financial freedom. She is now a prolific property investor who has built a real estate portfolio worth over £15m. Elizabeth holds a BA Honours in Business and Finance, a Chartered Banker Diploma and is a qualified CEMAP Mortgage Broker. Today, Elizabeth is still an active investor but spends most of her time mentoring and advising others who desire to begin their own journey to creating wealth through successful property investment. Her first book, *The 5 W's of Wealth Creation*, has proven successful in equipping people with the necessary principles to create wealth. It is Elizabeth's desire that everyone accesses the wealth creation seed within them. Her story is one of honesty, growth and hard work. Her second book, *Successful Property Investment* is a must read for anyone seeking the fundamental truths needed to achieve success in property investment.

FOOTNOTES

1. Hemple, Peter. "What impact will higher stamp duty charges have on buy-to-let?"p27,http://www.property-investor-news.com/news/uk_news/2015/11/26/what_impact_will_higher_stamp_duty_charges_have_on_buytolet.html#.Vouo1lSLRdg, 26 Nov 2015

2. Arends, Bret. "Why Donald Trump is rich and you're not" http://www.marketwatch.com/story/why-donald-trump-is-rich-and-youre-not-2015-07-27, 27 Jul 2015

3. Sopory, Shivani. "6 Key Factors that Propel Successful Women Etrepreneurs"http://women2.com/2015/11/02/female-entrepreneurship-success/?hvid=2FTzA7&utm_source=Women+2.0+Mailing+List&utm_campaign=be128094c0-08-24-15_Weekly_Newsletter&utm_medium=email&utm_term=0_8e8e6a075d-be128094c0-305201265, 2 Nov 2015

4. 1 Kings 17:7-16

5. 2 Kings 4:1-7

PERSONAL NOTES

www.ingramcontent.com/pod-product-compliance
Lightning Source LLC
Chambersburg PA
CBHW071033080526
44587CB00015B/2595